CONTENTS

07 SESSION 1

27 SESSION 2

49 SESSION 3

65 SESSION 4

93 FAQ

WELCOME
WELCOME
WELCOME

We pray as you join us for this journey, you'll discover how to share Jesus more confidently with your family, friends, co-workers and others around you.

The Bible teaches us there is only one way to the Father, and that is through Jesus. However, there are many ways to Jesus. Your story is just one of those.

Over the next four sessions, we will explore His story, your story and how to share Jesus more confidently with others through your story. You will be equipped in understanding His role and your role, and we will answer some frequently asked questions.

We look forward to hearing your incredible testimonies of how 'sharing Jesus confidently' has impacted someone you've shared with.

SCAN QR CODE FOR VIDEOS

Sharing Jesus Confidently 2025
All materials contained in this book are the property of Sharing Jesus Confidently. To reproduce, republish, post, modify, distribute or display material from this publication, you must first obtain permission from the author at:

Sharee Rice
Abbottsford, Victoria
Melbourne, Australia 3067

sharee@shareerice.com

Published & Distributed by: Sharee Rice Ministries
ISBN: 978-0-6457377-2-1

Writing by Sharee Rice
Formatting and pre-press by Sharee Rice Ministries
Printed in Australia, USA & United Kingdom.

1
HOW TO SHARE HIS STORY

FACILITATOR TIPS

SESSION 01
KEY FOCUSES

5 GOSPEL POINTS
A simple way for someone to outline Jesus' story & why it is relevant.

4 GOSPEL TRUTHS
The four Gospel truths derive from John 3:16 and are 4 ways to simply share the Gospel with an individual.

TIP 1

Introduce session 1 by emphasizing that the purpose of the chapter is that participants would understand what they need to communicate when sharing 'His story'. It can be easy for session 1 to become 'white noise' to participants who are well acquainted with the gospel message if they do not understand the purpose of the session, being 'simple articulation' of the Gospel.

TIP 2

Discuss the importance of making disciples through evangelism – correlate Henry Martyn's statement to the discussion. Ask your group what discipleship means to them.

TIP 3

Pause once the 4 Gospel truths have been unveiled and discuss with your group the need for non-believers to understand this model – break it down again and remind them that an easy way to remember it is - 'what God has done', and 'Man's response'.

TIP 4

At the end of session 1, re-visit the 5 Gospel points as well as the 4 Gospel truths. Ask your group to recite them.

HIS HEART

The closer we follow Jesus and the more we are in love with Him, the more we will understand His heart and His desire for the lost to be found.

HIS COMMAND

The Great Commission

"The Spirit of Christ is the Spirit of Missions, and the nearer we get to Him the more intensely missionary we must become"

HENRY MARTYN

Therefore making disciples is not optional.

And Jesus came and said to them, "All authority in heaven and on earth has been given to Me. Go therefore and make disciples of all nations, baptizing them in the name of the Father and of the Son and of the Holy Spirit, teaching them to observe all that I have commanded you. And behold, I am with you always, to the end of the age."

MATTHEW 28:18-20

We believe the Great Commission is not the "great option" but rather "our mission". It's not an add on feature. It's not a once off activity. It's not an event added to the calendar or a program you complete for extra credit.

This is the foundational Kingdom culture value we find throughout scripture that making disciples is not optional.

FACILITATOR NOTES: These notes will help you guide your group through this course. You can also add your own notes as you go through the course to where and what areas you think may need a focus.

1. What does 'making disciples is not optional' mean to you? How can you make disciples in your everyday life?

OUR LIFESTYLE

We believe that every Christian should be discipling at least one person. It's the trademark of a follower of Jesus, and the very example He left for us to follow.

Evangelism is a natural overflow of the Christian life, and it is a spiritual discipline, that needs to be practiced.

Mission is not what we do, it's who we are.

FACILITATOR NOTES:

1. Focus on the "one." Ask the question: Are you discipling one person? Who? How? e.g., building relationship, praying for them, inviting them to church.

WHAT IS HIS STORY?

 **GOD IS HOLY**

MAN IS A SINNER

MAN NEEDS A SAVIOUR
JESUS IS THAT SAVIOUR

JESUS CAME, LIVED, DIED, AND ROSE AGAIN

JESUS IS COMING BACK

"I AM A SINNER SAVED BY GRACE."

What does this statement mean to someone who doesn't know Jesus yet?
His story in 5 simple steps.

GOD IS HOLY
God has created us to worship and be in relationship with Him.

Everyone who is called by My name, whom I created for My glory, whom I formed and made.
ISAIAH 43:7

Know that the Lord is God. It is He who made us, and we are His.
PSALM 100:3

I am the LORD your God; consecrate yourselves and be holy, because I am holy. Do not make yourselves unclean by any creature that moves along the ground.
LEVITICUS 11:44

MAN IS A SINNER
We are fallen
- We have all sinned
  ROMANS 3:23
- While we were weak, Christ died for the ungodly
  ROMANS 5:6
- Sin separates us from God
  ISAIAH 59:2
- The wages of sin is death
  ROMANS 6:23

FACILITATOR NOTES:
1. Discuss, 'God has created us for relationship' with him. What does this look like in our lives?
2. Read out Isaiah 43:7 and Psalm 100:3 together with your group.

What is Sin?

The wrong things that you and I do. Anything that doesn't please the heart of God and goes against our conscience.

Sin isn't just something we do, Sin is also a noun.
The problem isn't just our sinning. The problem is that we were born sinners. The reason we were born sinners is not because of anything we did. It is because of who we are related to – Adam and Eve.

Behold, the Lamb of God, who takes away the sin of the world
JOHN 1:29

MAN NEEDS A SAVIOUR
JESUS IS THAT SAVIOUR

Salvation is found in Jesus.
We need a saviour because we can't save ourselves from sin. Jesus is that saviour because He was the only one who could pay that price on our behalf.

There is no other name by which mankind can be saved
ACTS 4:12

For God so loved the world that He gave His only son, that whoever believes in Him shall not perish but have eternal life
JOHN 3:16

FACILITATOR NOTES:
1. Discuss what is not Christ-like behaviour.
2. Who knows the verse John 3:16?

JESUS CAME, LIVED, DIED FOR US, AND ROSE AGAIN

He came, lived, died for us and rose again. He conquered sin, death and the grave.

> "But God demonstrates His own love for us in this; while we were still sinners, Christ died for us."
>
> ROMANS 5:8

> "In Him, we have redemption through His blood, the forgiveness for our trespasses, according to the riches of His grace, which He lavished upon us."
>
> EPHESIANS 1:7

> For I delivered to you as of first importance what I also received: that Christ died for our sins in accordance with the Scriptures, that He was buried, that He was raised on the third day in accordance with the Scriptures, and that He appeared to Cephas, then to the twelve. Then He appeared to more than five hundred brothers at one time, most of whom are still alive, though some have fallen asleep. Then He appeared to James, then to all the apostles. Last of all, as to one untimely born, He appeared also to me.
>
> 1 CORINTHIANS 15:3-8

By laying down His life for us, He paid for all of our sins, making the pathway to salvation available to everyone.

FACILITATOR NOTES:

1. Discuss why? What are the reasons? People want to know why He is coming back again.
- Enjoy eternity with Him.
- No tears, pain or suffering.
- We wouldn't know how amazing eternal life with Him is.

- Read the verses above with your group. Ask others to read. Encourage the group to use these five simple steps to help in sharing the gospel.

"Christ redeemed us from the curse of the law by becoming a curse for us."

GALATIANS 3:13

Jesus came as a man and lived on this earth, conquering sin, death and the grave when He went to the cross and rose again.

JESUS PROMISES US THAT HE WILL COME BACK AGAIN.

"And if I go and prepare a place for you, I will come again and will take you to myself, that where I am you may be also."

JOHN 14:3

Session 01

YOU KNOW IT'S GOD'S HEART THAT ALL MEN MIGHT BE SAVED.

THE LORD IS NOT SLOW IN KEEPING HIS PROMISE, AS SOME UNDERSTAND SLOWNESS. INSTEAD HE IS PATIENT WITH YOU, NOT WANTING ANYONE TO PERISH, BUT EVERYONE TO COME TO REPENTANCE."

2 PETER 3:9

LET'S KEEP IT SIMPLE

We can often overcomplicate the Gospel message in sharing Jesus with people. "Evangelism is less of a technique and more of a lifestyle, from a place of understanding." It's not time to show off your theology but to keep it simple!

HOW DO WE SHARE IT SIMPLY?

An easy way to share this with someone is to break it down into four truths. Two truths are about what God has done for us and the other two are our response. This is based on a well know bible verse, John 3:16

FOR GOD SO LOVED THE WORLD, THAT HE GAVE HIS ONLY SON, THAT WHOEVER BELIEVES IN HIM SHOULD NOT PERISH BUT HAVE ETERNAL LIFE'.

JOHN 3:16

FACILITATOR NOTES:

1. Read through the verses together as a group. What are the four things we receive when we respond to the Gospel? Share the four gospel points with someone.

TAKE TIME TO UNDERSTAND THESE TRUTHS, TO HELP SHARE HIS STORY WITH SOMEONE.

WHAT GOD HAS DONE AND MAN'S RESPONSE TO IT

WHAT GOD HAS DONE:

GOD LOVED

God so **loved** the world.
JOHN 3:16

Greater love has no one than this, that someone lay down his life for his friends.
JOHN 15:13

GOD GAVE

He **gave** His Son
JOHN 3:16

but God shows His love for us in that while we were still sinners, Christ died for us.
ROMANS 5:8

For by grace you have been saved through faith. And this is not your own doing; it is the gift of God, not a result of works, so that no one may boast.
EPHESIANS 2:8-9

FACILITATOR NOTES:

MAN'S RESPONSE TO THIS IS:

YOU BELIEVE

Whoever **believes** ...
Jesus died and rose again.
JOHN 3:16

WHAT IS IT WE BELIEVE?

- Jesus is the Son of God
- He came and lived in this world
- He died on a cross
- Price was paid for sin
- He rose again 3 days later
- Victory over death and the grave
- We have eternal with Him
- He is coming back again

YOU RECEIVE

- Forgiveness of sins
- Right standing with God
- The right to become a child of God
- Eternal life (everlasting)
- Right to receive the Holy Spirit

FORGIVENESS OF SINS

And Peter said to them, "Repent and be baptized every one of you in the name of Jesus Christ for the forgiveness of your sins, and you will receive the gift of the Holy Spirit.
ACTS 2:38

RIGHT TO BECOME A CHILD OF GOD

But to all who did receive Him, who believed in His name, He gave the right to become children of God.
JOHN 1:12

RIGHT STANDING (RIGHTEOUSNESS)

"For if, because of one man's trespass, death reigned through that one man, much more will those who receive the abundance of grace and the free gift of righteousness reign in life through the one man Jesus Christ.
ROMANS 5:17

ETERNAL LIFE

Everyone who calls on the name of the Lord will be saved.
ROMANS 10:13

RIGHT TO RECEIVE THE HOLY SPIRIT

"And when he had said this, he breathed on them and said to them, "Receive the Holy Spirit."
JOHN 20:22

These four truths have most likely changed your life at some point and changed my life at some point. When we break it down this simply and share it with our friends, it will be guaranteed to change their life.

God loved and God gave, He did all that was needed and what we do in response is believe and receive – how awesome is that!

© Sharee Rice

Session 01 | 23

QUESTIONS:

The Great Commission is not an add-on feature, it is to be part of our lifestyle. Discuss this statement.

Why can it be hard to use the word "sin" in our politically correct world?

What are the five simple steps to understanding the Gospel?

QUESTIONS:

What are the four simple truths of the gospel from John 3:16?

Extra Writing Space:

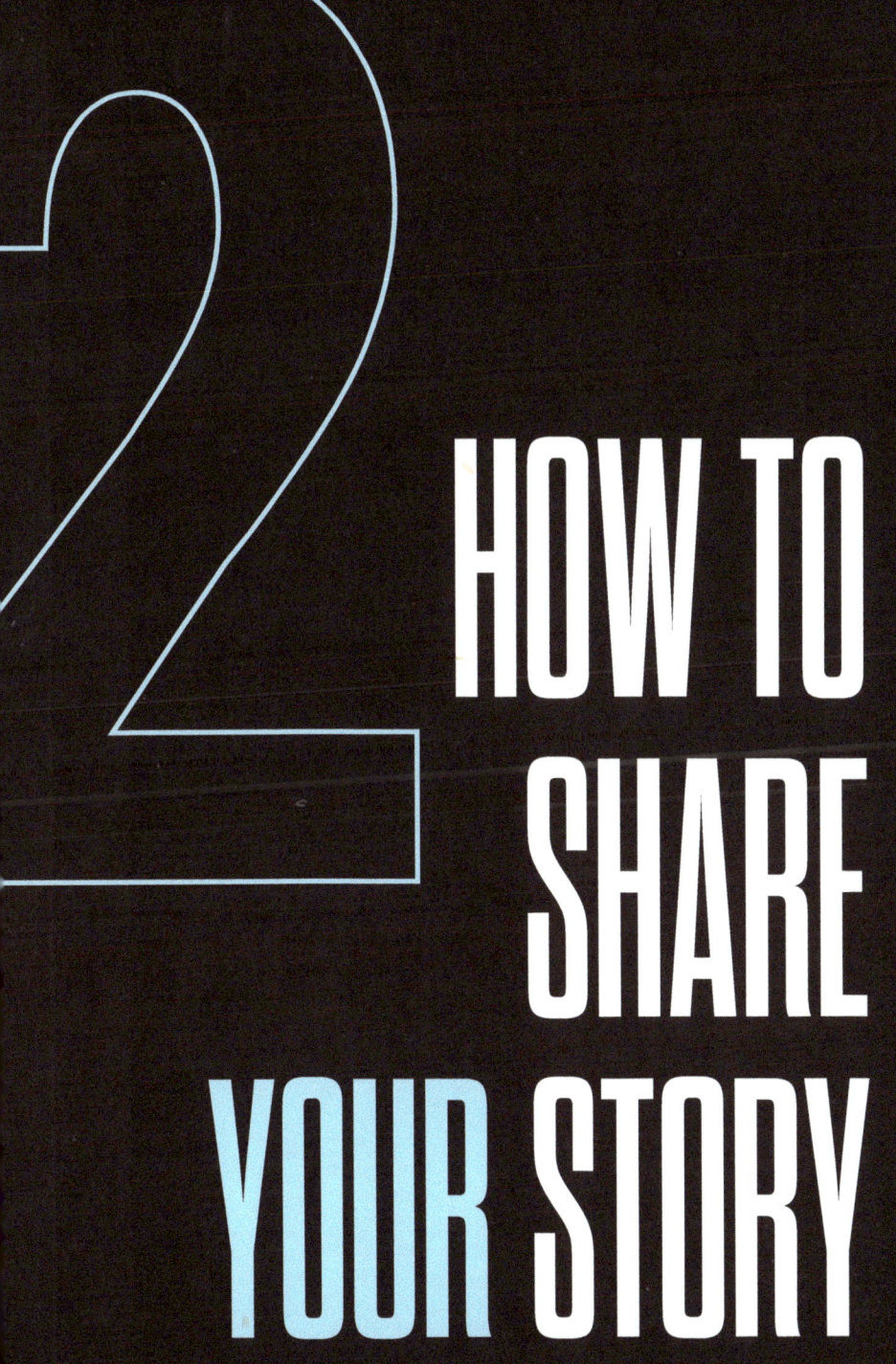

2 HOW TO SHARE YOUR STORY

FACILITATOR TIPS

SESSION 02
KEY FOCUSES

HOW TO CONSTRUCT A TIMELINE
How a person can share their story by using a timeline of before Christ, when they met Christ, and after Christ.

TIPS WHEN SHARING
How to get the most out of your story.

TIP 1
Introduce session 2. A good way to introduce session 2 is by recapping session 1 and the correlation that session 2 will have with session 1. I.e., "Session 2 is all about learning how to intersect chapter 1 (His story) with your story". Then introduce what you will be covering in session 2.

© Sharee Rice

TIP 2
Re-visit the story of the woman at the well and use it as an example of how His story intersects with ours. Open a discussion with your group about the 'normality' of Jesus' conversation with the woman and how conversations about Jesus can be a part of everyday life.

TIP 3
Key Activity - Pause once the timeline of your story (life before Jesus, the moment I met Jesus, life with Jesus) has been introduced. Get your group to create a timeline of their story and add key moments of their faith journey on their timeline. Explain how the final state should contrast the initial state.

ie.

Life Before Jesus (BC)   **Moment I met Christ (MC)**   **After Christ (AC)**

TIP 4
At the conclusion of session 2, get your group to reflect on their story. Ask a few members to share their quick 'counter version' (1-3 mins) of their story to the rest of the group. Help guide them by sharing your story.

TIP 5
Remind your group how they can share their timeline by giving them the cheat code of 'BC, MC, AC'. This will help them remember how to share their story.

TIP 6
At the conclusion of the session, challenge each of them to share their story throughout the week. When your group gathers again, ask them for testimonies. Get them thinking about the 3 different versions of sharing their story and ask them to ponder how they would approach this over the week.

© Sharee Rice

STORIES ARE POWERFUL

Jesus loved to connect with others through stories when He walked the earth. He would tell stories and create stories through His life and ministry. His storytelling was directly linked to changing lives.

The power of a shared story can see towns, communities and people around us transformed.

Your story has power.

HOW TO SHARE YOUR STORY

Understanding how your story intersects with His story will help you share Jesus more confidently with others. Many people are ready to respond to the Gospel, they just don't know how. Our role is to share our story and provide regular opportunities to allow others to engage with the good news of Jesus Christ.

THE POWER OF A SHARED STORY

**The woman at the well
John 1:1-42**

In this story, we see Jesus meet a woman at the well. He engages with her in a normal conversation and asks her for a drink. As He engages with her, He brings her to a revelation of who He is in one simple encounter.

This one encounter completely changes this woman's life. She walks away never to be the same again. He revealed her whole life to her, and as a result, she knew He was the Messiah.

Her testimony impacted her community and many wanted to discover Jesus for themselves. Their lives were forever changed as a result.

This is the impact that your story can have on the people around you. Telling your story is a great way to connect His story to the lives of others around you.

Understanding your story is powerful and is key in being able to share Jesus more confidently.

Her story made way for His story to intersect other peoples lives.

FACILITATOR NOTES:

1. Recap session 1
- 5 Gospel points.
- 4 Truths.
- Ask your group to think about their story.
- What things can point others to Jesus?

> Many Samaritans from that town believed in Him because of the woman's testimony, "He told me all that I ever did." So when the Samaritans came to Him, they asked Him to stay with them, and he stayed there two days. And many more believed because of His word. They said to the woman, "It is no longer because of what you said that we believe, for we have heard for ourselves, and we know that this is indeed the Saviour of the world."
>
> JOHN 4:39-42

> And so it was with me, brothers and sisters. When I came to you, I did not come with eloquence or human wisdom as I proclaimed to you the testimony about God. For I resolved to know nothing while I was with you except Jesus Christ and Him crucified. I came to you in weakness with great fear and trembling. My message and my preaching were not with wise and persuasive words, but with a demonstration of the Spirit's power, so that your faith might not rest on human wisdom, but on God's power.
>
> We do, however, speak a message of wisdom among the mature, but not the wisdom of this age or of the rulers of this age, who are coming to nothing.
>
> 1 CORINTHIANS 2:1-6

SO, WHAT IS YOUR STORY?

HOW TO BUILD YOUR STORY AND SHARE THE GOSPEL MESSAGE

STEP 1

PART OF A BIGGER STORY

Most people enjoy hearing good stories. We love action, drama, conflict, quest, resolution, twists, the hero and the emotions of entering into a well told story.

The Bible says in 1 Peter 3:15 *"But in your hearts revere Christ as Lord. Always be prepared to give an answer to everyone who asks you to give the reason for the hope that you have. But do this with gentleness and respect."*

So, what is your story? What has your journey looked like with Jesus? Your story may or may not be an epic tale of cinematic proportions. Either way, that's perfectly ok. The purpose of your story is to point people to Christ and to show *His story* through *your story*.

Your story could be:
- A moment in time.
- A challenge.
- A miracle.
- An answered prayer.
- A negative turned into a positive.
- A divine moment with family or friends.
- Your encounter with Jesus.

Remember, it's all about Jesus. Show how *His story* has impacted your story. Then use *your story* to point others to Jesus

Session 02 35

STEP 2

WHAT MAKES A GOOD STORY?

Consider when and where you were born, the house you grew up in, even the school you attended. What was your family like? Any achievements in your life? Challenges? Highs? Lows? Turning points? These are just some examples that will help formulate your story. Draw a timeline to mark the events. Draw it as a graph plotting the highs, lows and turning points.

BIRTH **TODAY**

◄───►

When did you encounter Jesus? What amazes you about Jesus? What impact has He had on your life? How could these questions help point others to a relationship with Jesus? What are some key Bible verses that have encouraged you and helped you grow in your walk as a Christian?

You may want to map these out as points: before Christ, when you met Christ, and after Christ. There is a lot to cover! Remember that different parts of your story may connect with different people. The aim is to be prepared to give a reason for the hope that you have.

FACILITATOR NOTES: PAGES 28-29

1. Encourage everyone to think about these key moments of their faith journey and spend a few minutes writing them down.

STEP 3

LET'S GET STARTED

Reflect on the five helpful tips that are shared in the video and the following plan to help you get started.

POINTING TO JESUS' STORY WITH YOUR STORY

LIFE BEFORE JESUS

Beginning – Who you are, a brief look at you and what life was like before Jesus. Set up the story!

1.

2.

3.

THE MOMENT I MET JESUS

Middle – What was the problem? What needed to change? What were the issues you were facing alone?

1. _____

2. _____

3. _____

LIFE WITH JESUS

Ending – What was the outcome when you invited Jesus in? What changed? Conclude the story, set up the invitation.

1. _____

2. _____

3. _____

Pick a significant moment in your story, write it down, read it out loud, prepare yourself for people's responses, have a call to action, share it and record it. People can't argue with your story or your experience!

Next step is to learn when and how to share your story. There are three main versions of your story which will help share your story in different situations.

Counter version | 3 minutes
Eg. When paying for petrol or at the supermarket checkout.

Street version | 15 minutes
Eg. School drop off.

Café version | 30 minutes
Eg. Having a coffee with a friend at the café.

1) Write out Your story in approximately 300-500 words (300 words = 3 mins etc.).

Create three versions to help with various scenarios. Remember evangelism is a conversation it's not a presentation.

'BE PREPARED'
Think through any questions that may arise in response to your story and how you would answer.

PRAYER

Thank God for the Good News of Jesus. Pray that your story will be received in a mighty way.

Remember 1 Corinthians 2:1-6 says:

Proclaim Christ not with wise words but with a demonstration of the Spirits power.

FACILITATOR NOTES:

1. Give your group some time to reflect on their timeline. Ask some people in your group to share some things they have added to their timeline.

DON'T TRY TO BE SOMEONE ELSE. BE YOU.

The world doesn't need more copies. They need authentic individuals. Let God use you and your story through your personality to share His story. **He created you on purpose for His purpose.**

The writer of Thessalonians encourages us to see that it is not about what we say or how we say it. It is about being ready to share the Gospel in our own lives with other people.

You are unique, and your journey is unique. When you learn to share your story and the Gospel from this place, it will always flow authentically and genuinely.

THINK ABOUT THE 'PERSON' BEFORE YOU SPEAK 'RELIGION'

WHAT DRIVES YOU?
- It was love and compassion that saw Jesus through the cross.
- It should be love and compassion that drives us to share our story.

HELPFUL INTERSECTIONS:
- Look for common ground.
- Where does their story intersect with *His story* and *Your story*?

WHAT'S YOUR APPROACH?
- Be natural.
- Be genuine.
- Be authentic.
- Start with feeling and go after human connection.

WHAT'S YOUR LANGUAGE?
- Use language that people can relate to.
- Talk about Jesus in present tense.
- Don't be afraid to talk about your sin.

For our appeal does not spring from error or impurity or any attempt to deceive, but just as we have been approved by God to be entrusted with the gospel, so we speak, not to please man, but to please God who tests our hearts.

For we never came with words of flattery, as you know, nor with a pretext for greed—God is witness. Nor did we seek glory from people, whether from you or from others, though we could have made demands as apostles of Christ.

But we were gentle among you, like a nursing mother taking care of her own children.

So, being affectionately desirous of you, we were ready to share with you not only the gospel of God but also our own selves, because you had become very dear to us

1 THESSALONIANS 2:4-8

FACILITATOR NOTES:

1. Ask your group to share some things that drive them to share with others.
- Ask some questions about how we can be authentic What are some different ways we can approach people or situations?
- What are some examples of language we should avoid using?

TIPS

1 BE OPEN AND HONEST

Don't hide your hurt or excitement. Don't generalise your experience. Honest details are what make stories captivating. Your story should have pieces of defeat, victory, and the uphill battle of the messy middle. Be transparent. By being honest, you create a connection for people to identify themselves in your story. Share openly. Share honestly.

4 OFFER AN INVITATION

One of the best parts of a good story is the ending. It doesn't have to end nice and neat but you could make an invitation for implementation. You could encourage them to do what you did. Have a think what you could invite them to do. Often asking a question is helpful, i.e. "Have you ever experienced anything like this?" or "Would you like to?".

2

MAKE JESUS THE CENTRE

Make Jesus the hero of your story. Jesus is the character that provides comfort, victory, protection, sanity, clarity, etc.
Consider the role that Jesus played in your story. Make His actions and presence clear through regular words. He might work through someone in your story but be sure Jesus gets the credit; not you, not someone else.

3

BE BRIEF BUT COMPLETE

Yes, your story is important, however, you'll need to condense your '45 minute' monologue into an impactful 3-5 minutes. Think beginning, middle and end. Pick one specific moment. Craft the story. Make it clear, complete, and compelling. Get your story down to less than 5 minutes.

5

RELAX AND ENJOY THE EXPERIENCE!

The thought of sharing might feel daunting and uncomfortable so it's really important to remember what the objective is and keep going. Relax, enjoy and have some fun! It might take a while but it'll be worth it when you see people connect with your story. People will find your story inspiring, intriguing, or at the very least informative. No one is going to take offense by hearing your story. Don't preach. Don't try to convince, just share. Stories carry truth really well. Jesus did it all the time.

QUESTIONS:

SHARING
CONFIDENTLY

Review the story of the woman at the well and list some things in your own life that can point others to Jesus.

_____
_____
_____
_____
_____
_____
_____

Review the tips to help share your story and explain how you can apply these to your story. (eg. Be open and honest, make Jesus the centre, be brief but complete, offer an invitation, relax and enjoy).

_____
_____
_____
_____
_____
_____
_____

What amazes you about Jesus? How has knowing Jesus had an impact on your life?

_____
_____
_____
_____
_____
_____
_____

© Sharee Rice

QUESTIONS:

Spend some time before session three writing down your story using the guide in this session.

3

WHAT IS HIS ROLE?

When we share the Gospel, it's important to understand what His (Holy Spirit's) role is. Understanding that the Holy Spirit plays a big part in working through you, through the person you're sharing with, and the places He leads you to, helps us to partner with Him to bring transformation.

FACILITATOR TIPS

SESSION 03
KEY FOCUSES

UNDERSTANDING THE ROLE OF THE HOLY SPIRIT
- In you (Boldness)
- In them (Conviction)
- In cities & families (Transformation)

© Sharee Rice

TIP 1
Introduce session 3 by giving an overview of the 3 areas that you will cover. I.e., "In this session we will be covering the role of the Holy Spirit in 3 areas – in you, in them and in cities".

TIP 2
Provoke discussion. We want session 3 to be a real 'faith-building' session, with impartation through prayer.

TIP 3
Discuss; "Boldness & Power go hand-in-hand" (5:50 on video). Pause & ask your group what that means to them. Ask them for an example or time where they had seen the two working together.

TIP 4
Ask your group to share a testimony of a time when the Holy Spirit led them to the right person. This will help build faith in others to step-out.

TIP 5
Activity Pray - at the end of the session spend time praying for an impartation of boldness. Pray into destinies, that the Lord would place cities in the hearts of people in your group.

ADDITIONAL EXERCISES/PRAYER MINISTRY
Split into small groups and get your groups to pray over the lost.

Pray for;
- The Holy Spirit to convict the lost in their world,
- A baptism of the Holy Spirit and a move of power,
- Your city

WHAT IS THE ROLE OF THE HOLY SPIRIT

Mark 5:1-20
We read the story of a man who was possessed and tormented by demons, nothing in the natural could hold him, not even chains or shackles, no one could subdue him, and nothing could help him.

The Bible says that Jesus came through this part of town, and that possessed man came and fell at the feet of Jesus. The demons in him asked Jesus what He wanted with them, Jesus commanded the unclean spirits to come out of him.

In verse 15, we read:
A crowd soon gathered around Jesus, and they saw the man who had been possessed by the legion of demons. He was sitting there fully clothed and perfectly sane, and they were all afraid.

JESUS DID THE SUPERNATURAL WORK IN THIS MAN'S LIFE

The man was healed, restored into the community, and became a witness for Jesus in his community.

THE ROLE OF THE HOLY SPIRIT

In this section we will look at the Role of the Holy Spirit;
- In you – **Boldness.**
- In them – **Conviction.**
- In cities - **Transformation.**

FACILITATOR NOTES:

1. Encourage your group to share the short version of their testimony from the session 2 framework. If no one in your group wants to share, you could share your own story.

2. Discuss and read through the story of the demon possessed man. What was humanity's role and what was the Holy Spirit's role?

Session 03 | 53

THE ROLE OF THE HOLY SPIRIT IN YOU

Power to be a witness

But you will receive power when the Holy Spirit has come upon you, and you will be my witnesses
ACTS 1:8

The Holy Spirit working in you is the power for you to be a witness.

A **Witness** is someone who testifies about something they know or have seen. To give your testimony is to give evidence. Literally meaning; your testimony is to give evidence, of what you have seen, heard and know. Your story is an experience that gives testimony to the goodness and grace of God.

The Holy Spirit gives you power to be a witness, because it's not about how much of the Holy Spirit we have but how much the Holy Spirit has of us.

Found people, find people

The Gospel is communicated to 'lost people' by 'saved people'.

"Your story is a powerful testimony to the goodness and Gospel of Jesus. The role of the Holy Spirit is to empower you to share that."

THE ROLE OF THE HOLY SPIRIT IN YOU

There is only one thing you can't do in heaven and that is to tell people about Jesus.

BOLDNESS

The one thing required to tell people on Earth about Jesus is boldness.

The Holy Spirit will give you both power and boldness. Boldness is something that will overtake you. It is described through the Greek word as a lucid and daring statement – telling it all – freedom in speaking, unreservedness in speech and being open and frank, fearless and confident.

"But the righteous are as bold as a lion."
PROVERBS 28:1

Boldness is not arrogance, the loudest person in the room or being controversial for the sake of being controversial.

"Now, when they saw the boldness of Peter and John and perceived that they were uneducated, common men, they were astonished. And they recognised that they had been with Jesus."
ACTS 4:13

FACILITATOR NOTES:

1. Has anyone experienced boldness in sharing about Jesus? Discuss with your group.

THE ROLE OF THE HOLY SPIRIT IN YOU

Boldness is the Spirit-given conviction that we must speak about what we have seen and heard.

"For we, on our part, cannot stop telling [people] about what we have seen and heard."
ACTS 4:20

Boldness and power go hand-in-hand and we can have confidence in knowing we don't need to worry about what to say as the Holy Spirit will tell us.

We can have confidence in this
- He gives us power.
- Boldness.
- The words to speak.

"The Holy Spirit will teach you in that very hour what you ought to say."
LUKE 12:11-12

FACILITATOR NOTES:

1. Encourage your group not to be afraid to share if they feel that God is leading them to. Give an example or a personal experience.

THE ROLE OF THE HOLY SPIRIT IN THEM

CONVICTION

"And when He comes, He will convict the world concerning sin and righteousness and judgement."
JOHN 16:8

Holy Spirit convicts humanity of sin, righteousness and judgement.

It is not our role to convince anyone, and it's not any form of manipulation by man; instead it is the work of the Holy Spirit, at work in someone else's life, bringing conviction and awareness of sin.

"Because our gospel came to you not only in word but also in power and in the Holy Spirit and with full conviction."
1 THESSALONIANS 1:5

Your personality may attract people, your knowledge may impress people, your words may stir people, and your pleading may cause people to respond, but it is the Holy Spirit convicts and saves people.

"And no one can say Jesus is Lord except in the Holy Spirit."
1 CORINTHIANS 12:3

THE ROLE OF THE HOLY SPIRIT IN THEM

"When Holy God draws near in true revival people come down under terrible conviction of sin. The outstanding feature of spiritual awakening has been the profound consciousness of the presence and holiness of God"

HENRY BLACKABY

THE ROLE OF THE HOLY SPIRIT IN CITIES

TRANSFORMATION

The Holy Spirit moves across people, families, and communities, leading them to transformation. You can trust that whoever you are directed to by the Holy Spirit, He is already at work in their life!

The Holy Spirit will guide you to the right person or people group.

Phillip was led to the Ethiopian Eunuch.

ACTS 8:26-35

Holy Spirit led Peter to the awareness of three men he was to go with.

ACTS 10:19-22

Holy Spirit kept Paul from preaching in Asia and sent him to Macedonia.

ACTS 16:6-7

Whilst praying, Paul ends up in a trance. He saw the Lord speaking and is instructed to leave Jerusalem.

ACTS 22:17-18

FACILITATOR NOTES:

1. Read through these verses with your group. Ask others to find the verse and read it out to the group.

© Sharee Rice

Whoever you share with, Jesus has already laid down His life for. And the Holy Spirit is, and always will be, more invested in them than we ever could be.

He's also invested in their families, communities, and He desires that schools, universities, cities, and many nations be transformed.

FAMILIES

One who heard us was a woman named Lydia, from the city of Thyatira, a seller of purple goods, who was a worshiper of God. The Lord opened her heart to pay attention to what was said by Paul. And after she was baptized, and her household as well.

ACTS 16:15

Then he brought them out and said, "Sirs, what must I do to be saved?" And they said, "Believe in the Lord Jesus, and you will be saved, you and your household." And they spoke the word of the Lord to him and to all who were in his house. And he took them the same hour of the night and washed their wounds; and he was baptized at once, he and his family.

ACTS 16:30-34

THE ROLE OF THE HOLY SPIRIT IN CITIES

CITIES

The next Sabbath, almost the whole city gathered to hear the word of the Lord.

ACTS 13:44

God has placed you in families and has intended for your family, community, city, state, and nations of the world to be impacted by Jesus through your life, story, and the Good News.

PRAY FOR WHERE GOD HAS SENT YOU.

"But seek the welfare of the city where I have sent you into exile, and pray to the Lord on its behalf, for in its welfare you will find your welfare."

JEREMIAH 29:4-7

"True revival should affect the cities where we live."

And Jesus came and said to them, "All authority in heaven and on earth has been given to me. Go therefore and make disciples of all nations, baptizing them in the name of the Father and of the Son and of the Holy Spirit, teaching them to observe all that I have commanded you. And behold, I am with you always, to the end of the age."

MATTHEW 28:18-20

QUESTIONS:

What are some things you can do to become bold in sharing the gospel with others?

___

What role do our personalities and knowledge play in people responding to the gospel?

___

What is the role of the Holy Spirit in the unbeliever?

___

© Sharee Rice

QUESTIONS:

Who has the Holy Spirit been leading you to? God put you in families and has intent for your family, community and city, state, nations of the world to be impacted by Jesus through your life, story and the good news.

4 WHAT IS YOUR ROLE?

FACILITATOR TIPS

SESSION 04
KEY FOCUSES

PRAY
The role of prayer & what to pray for

CARE
How to truly care for people

SHARE
Links back to session 1 & 2

INVITE
How to invite someone to Christ & lead them in a salvation prayer

© Sharee Rice

TIP 1
Emphasize & discuss the statement, "If we do the natural, Jesus will take care of the supernatural". This is a good way to transition from session 3, which is all about the Holy Spirit's role, into session 4, which is all about our role.

TIP 2
Key Activity When 'Care' is discussed, pause the chapter, and ask your group to commit to meeting a community need. Together select something that you would like to contribute toward.
This is a crucial exercise to incorporate into your chapter.

TIP 3
Ask if anyone in your group has a need. Activate 'care' within your own group.

TIP 4
In session 2 we encouraged people to share their story. On the back of that, challenge your group to go the next step and 'invite' somebody to know Christ. In a similar fashion to session 2, re visit this the next time you gather and see if anybody has a testimony.

TIP 5
Ask your group if they have any testimonies of a time when they extended an invitation and what the outcome was.

ADDITIONAL EXERCISE
Linking back to the 'care' component, have everyone pull out their phone and message someone something from the 'practical day-today' list in 'Care' section of the book, (thank someone, praise someone, offer to take them out for lunch, invite them over, ask them if there is anything they can pray for).

I.e., "Hi Don, I hope you are well. I just wanted to say how thankful I am to have such a great friend like you in my life. I love your authenticity. Let's go for a walk soon".

© Sharee Rice

WHAT IS YOUR ROLE?

In Mark 5:1-20, we read the story of the demon-possessed man; Jesus did a supernatural work in this man's life, we read that after his encounter with Jesus, he is "now seated in his right mind." and "fully clothed."

Jesus did a supernatural work in this man's life, he was sitting there fully clothed and perfectly sane.

When you read "fully clothed", have you ever wondered how?

Clothes did not just fall from heaven. Somebody dressed him, and somebody had to provide for him, we can assume somebody cleaned up his wounds and someone took the time to be with him.

Jesus does the supernatural but is looking for people to step in and do the natural.

"IF WE DO THE NATURAL, JESUS WILL TAKE CARE OF THE SUPERNATURAL"

There are four things that we can do to partner with God in what He is doing in the supernatural:

PRAY
CARE
SHARE
INVITE

Session 04 | 69

PRAY

THE ROLE OF PRAYER

"But seek the welfare of the city where I have sent you into exile, and pray to the Lord on its behalf, for in its welfare, you will find your welfare."
JEREMIAH 29:4-7

PRAY FOR WHERE GOD HAS SENT YOU

Our fight is not with the flesh but in the Spirit and we are to fight in the place of prayer.

For our struggle is not against flesh and blood, but against the rulers, against authorities, against the powers of this dark world and against the spiritual forces of evil in the heavenly realms[1]
EPHESIANS 6:12

PRAYER FUELS POWER

We often know that we should pray but don't know WHAT to pray for! God has given us the scriptures to pray over unbelievers and our city; here are the scriptures you can use and some examples of how you can pray.

FACILITATOR NOTES:
1. Go over this verse together and highlight what we are fighting for in prayer. "Prayer fuels power"

HOW TO PRAY FOR THEM

First of all then, I urge that supplications, prayers, intercessions, and thanksgiving be made for all people.

1 TIMOTHY 2:1

PRAYER EXAMPLE:

Jesus, I thank You for the people of my city, in my world, my family and friends. I thank You, Jesus, that You have given Your life for them so that they may come into a relationship with the Father.

Holy Spirit, I thank You that You are already at work in their life, and I open myself to be used by You to see the people of this city, my family and friends come to know You. Amen.

Pray for God to open their spiritual eyes.

In their case the god of this world has blinded the minds of the unbelievers to keep them from seeing the light of the Gospel of the glory of Christ, who is the image of God.

2 CORINTHIANS 4:4

Pray for God to give them ears to hear.

"For this people's heart has grown dull, and with their ears, they can barely hear, and their eyes they have closed, lest they should see with their eyes and hear with their ears and understand with their heart and turn, and I would heal them."

MATTHEW 13:15

PRAYER EXAMPLE:
Holy Spirit, I thank You for my friend/daughter/father/barista. I know You are already at work in their life. I ask You to reveal Yourself to them, lift the scales off their eyes, and open their ears to hear You speaking to them. In Jesus name, I pray. Amen.

Pray God gives them the faith to believe.
"Testifying both to Jews and Greeks of repentance toward God and of faith in our Lord Jesus Christ."
ACTS 20:21

Pray and ask God to give them the will to respond.
"Because, if you confess with your mouth that Jesus is Lord and believe in your heart that God raised him from the dead, you will be saved."
ROMANS 10:9

PRAYER EXAMPLE:
Holy Spirit, I pray that You would activate faith in their hearts and give them the will to respond to Your call. I pray that You would use the things in their life to draw closer to You, and they would see You in everything; causing their heart to engage with You.

FACILITATOR NOTES:

1. What can we pray for? (Recap the above). Ask anyone if they have experienced God working in these areas from a prayer they have prayed?

HOW TO PRAY FOR YOURSELF

Pray for personal obedience.
"Go out to the roads and country lanes and compel people to come in so that my house may be full."
LUKE 14:23

"Go make disciples of all nations, baptising them in the name of the Father, Son and Holy Spirit. Teaching them to obey all that I have commanded, and surely I am with you to the end of the age."
MATTHEW 28:19-20

Pray for opportunities to come and for clarity when you share.
"At the same time, pray also for us, that God may open to us a door for the word, to declare the mystery of Christ, on account of which I am in prison – that I may make it clear, which is how I ought to speak."
COLOSSIANS 4:3-4

Pray for the right words and for boldness as you speak.
"And also for me, that words may be given to me in opening my mouth boldly to proclaim the mystery of the gospel, for which I am an ambassador in chains, that I may declare it boldly, as I ought to speak."
EPHESIANS 6:19-20

FACILITATOR NOTES:
1. Break down these verses and what the Bible is encouraging us in how to pray.

© Sharee Rice

PRAYER EXAMPLE:
Holy Spirit, I pray that when I hear Your voice or Your prompting, that I would boldly obey. I pray that boldness will overcome any fear or hesitation.

I pray God for You to open up opportunities for me to share with my friends and family with clarity and boldness that can only come from You, the message of Jesus.

Holy Spirit will give you what to say

For the Holy Spirit will teach you in that very hour what you ought to say."

LUKE 12:12

God will provide you with the right words to speak, and if you ask, you will receive. *"You have not because you ask not."*

JAMES 4:2-3

PRAYER EXAMPLE:
Holy Spirit, would You fill my mouth with the right words to say, that my friends need to hear. I trust You, when I don't know what to say, that You will provide wisdom and revelation. I trust that You will lead me and that my words will be seeds that will not go to waste.

FACILITATOR NOTES:

1. Go over the things we can pray for ourselves. Ask if anyone has experienced any of these things from a prayer they have prayed (examples).

Pray that your words would be effective.

"Finally, brothers, pray for us that the word of the Lord may speed ahead and be honoured, as happened among you."
2 THESSALONIANS 3:1

EXAMPLE PRAYER:

I pray, Holy Spirit, that You take the words that I speak and cause them to be effective. I pray that my words aren't merely words but that they would pierce the heart, be received openly, and lead to a revelation of You.

FACILITATOR NOTES:

1. Remember that people will be encouraged when sharing life experience in this area.

PRAY FOR BOLDNESS

As you ask God for more opportunities, He will begin to open doors, and will grant you the boldness needed to be obedient.

Pray for words of boldness

Now, Lord, look upon their threats and grant to Your servants to continue to speak Your word with all boldness. Stretch out Your hand to heal, and signs and wonders are performed through the name of Your holy servant Jesus."

After they had prayed, the place in which they were gathered together was shaken, and they were all filled with the Holy Spirit and continued to speak the word of God with boldness.

ACTS 4:29-31

When we pray in the natural, it aligns us with what the Holy Spirit wants to do in the supernatural.

Results and power of praying for boldness

He began to speak boldly in the synagogue, but when Priscilla and Aquila heard him, they took him aside and explained to him the way of God more accurately.

ACTS 18:26

And he entered the synagogue for the next three months spoke boldly, reasoning and persuading them about the Kingdom of God.
ACTS 19:8

But though we had already suffered and been shamefully treated at Philippi, as you know, we had boldness in our God to declare to you the Gospel of God in the midst of much conflict.
1 THESSALONIANS 2:2

"WITHOUT THE HOLY SPIRIT'S BOLDNESS, OUR WORLD WOULD SIMPLY REMAIN UNREACHED."

CARE

CARE BEFORE YOU SHARE

"People don't care how much you know; they want to know how much you care."

STORY OF THE GOOD SAMARITAN

In Luke 10:25-37 Jesus shares the two greatest commands; *"Love the Lord your God… and to love your neighbour as yourself."*

Jesus paints a picture of what this looks like through a story. A man fell among robbers and was stripped and beaten and left lying on the side of the road.

Three people pass by this man, but only one person stopped and cared.

He is known as the Good Samaritan:
- He stops after seeing him and shows compassion.
- He goes to him.
- He goes the extra mile, takes him and places him in care, and pays for it.

This is how Jesus sums up how to care in this story by saying, **"Go and do likewise."**

DON'T JUST SAY IT; DO IT.

FACILITATOR NOTES:
1. Ask your group if they have an example of ways they have cared for someone before sharing with someone.

HOW CAN YOU SHOW PEOPLE YOU CARE?

Things you can look for in your conversations:
- "I am not going well"
  – experiencing struggles in life.
- "I am not ready or prepared for that"
  – surprises (eg. kids, family, job etc.)
- "I am not from here"
  – I just moved into the area.

When we hear any of these in our conversations, we should:

1. Slow down, be interested, ask yourself how you would feel in this situation, ask questions, be invested in people's lives even when it costs you.

2. Stop, have compassion, imagine yourself in their position, and ask yourself the question, what would I need in this situation?

3. Reach out to people, check in and see how they are doing. Take time to listen! Learn from Jesus. He never rushed past anyone.

4. Offer to help, meet a need, ask what they need. Be generous, go above and beyond.

> **YOU MAY NOT CHANGE THE WORLD AS ONE PERSON, BUT YOU CAN CHANGE THE WORLD OF ONE PERSON.**

BUILDING CARE INTO THE PRACTICAL DAY TO DAY THINGS THAT YOU DO:

- **Thank someone.**
  Show gratitude for their service or time.

- **Praise someone.**
  Send an encouraging message, compliment someone.

- **Pay for someone's** lunch/dinner/coffee/fuel/parking meter.

- **Help someone with a task**
  moving, carrying bags etc.

- **Host a meal for your neighbours.**
  Gather people who may be alone on special occasions like Christmas or Mothers day

- **Listen to someone.**

- **Pray for someone.**

"People who truly care won't have to tell you they care; they will show you they care. You will know them by their fruit."

SHOW YOU CARE BEFORE YOU SHARE.

FACILITATOR NOTES:

1. Talk and discuss the different ways we can hear and be guided by the Holy Spirit. Give examples in your own life.

2. Ask your group if they have experienced a moment of salvation in a friend or family member. Did they see God already working in them before the moment of salvation?

SHARE

It's simple and easy, and everyone can do it!

Share your story: before Christ, when you met Christ and after Christ.

Jesus is the greatest example of this; He shared stories and parables. Your story can do exactly this.

Tell your stroy and connect to His story. That will intersect with their story, then you can deliver the good news of Jesus.

HOW TO SHARE YOUR STORY

- **Your story:** point of need, I was looking for acceptance.
- **How Jesus met that in you:** I found it in Jesus, He set me free from seeking man's approval.
- **Present solution:** I have been set free from fear of man, and I have freedom in Jesus.
- **Ask the question:** Have you ever experienced this? or maybe you have felt like this?

> WE SHARE BECAUSE WE CARE

FACILITATOR NOTES:

1. Ask your group what things can help us connect with people?

2. Think of some examples you can share with your group about personal connections.

3. Arrange your group into pairs and ask them to share a short version of their story; they can practice asking these questions.

4. Ask your group if anyonw has an example of changing the way they share depending on the situation?

INVITE

He has put eternity into man's heart.
ECCLESIASTES 3:11

Invitations are personal, everybody loves to be included and invited into something good. When Jesus was first found in the gospels by people, it was an invitation that was given to come, that lead to many lives being changed. People are just waiting for an invitation.

God is looking for someone who will stand in the gap – that someone is you.

I looked for someone among them who would build up the wall and stand before me in the gap on behalf of the land so I would not have to destroy it, but I found no one.
EZEKIEL 22:30

Evangelism is simply moving someone one step closer to Jesus. Nathanael said to him, "Can anything good come out of Nazareth?" Philip said to him, "Come and see. So what is their next step?

How is this related to the person you are praying for? Could it be coffee? A dinner invitation? An invitation to a life group or church?

© Sharee Rice

REMEMBER THE STORY OF THE WOMAN AT THE WELL?

John 4:29, the woman says, "Come see a man who told me everything I ever did..."
Jesus acknowledges her sin and brokeness, but when she encounters Him, instead of receiving judgment, she encounters His grace and love. All she wants to do is invite people to experience what she has experienced – compassion, love, and grace.

"COME" IS THE GREATEST INVITATION TO GOD'S GRACE.

Her invitation led to so many others encountering Jesus.

Many came because of her invitation, but they believed because of His word - when they met Jesus.

Your friends may not believe because of what you share, but they may because you followed it up with an invitation.

Invitations are throughout the Bible and show us there is power in asking someone to respond, and we see the followers of Jesus inviting people to come and know Him.

© Sharee Rice

EXAMPLES OF INVITATION

Peter: Repent and be baptised
ACTS 2:38

Paul: Beg you to be reconciled
2 CORINTHIANS 5:20

Joshua: Calling people to commit
JOSHUA 24:14-16

Elijah: How long will you hesitate between two opinions?
1 KINGS 18:21

> THE GOOD NEWS OF THE GOSPEL IS AN INVITATION THAT REQUIRES A RESPONSE.

We are ambassadors for Christ, God making His appeal through us.

"We implore you, on behalf of Christ, to be reconciled to God. Behold, now is the favourable time; behold, now is the day of salvation."
2 CORINTHIANS 5:20 & 6:2

Today is that day of salvation.

It's an invitation, and WE need to GIVE that INVITATION. The Greatest invitation is to a relationship with Jesus, through God.

That which we have seen and heard we proclaim also to you, so that you too may have fellowship with us; and indeed our fellowship is with the Father and with his Son Jesus Christ.

1 JOHN 1:3

HOW TO GIVE AN INVITATION

We can engage people for a response by asking two of the greatest questions;

- **Have you ever?**
- **Would you like to?**

After you have shared a story or an experience, the questions above can help someone process what you have just shared. Asking someone, "have you experienced anything like this?" and following that up with, "would you like to?" can open up an invitation for them to know Jesus.

When people have seen & heard about Jesus, we can then confidently extend that invitation to them.

FACILITATOR NOTES:

1. Think and share some different ways you can tailor your questions to suit a situation.

Tailor your questions to suit the person you are sharing with, and varying your response to their response is essential.

TESTIMONY

A few years ago, I met a young woman at a conference who I discovered lived in the same small town as me growing up.

She had come to know Jesus as an adult, and while talking at this conference, many years later, we discovered that I was pastoring the youth in that town when she was at school there.

When she realised this, she said to me, "are you telling me that there was a church in our town where I could have found Jesus as a teenager, and no one ever invited me?"

- PS SHAREE RICE

All it takes is an invitation!

If you step out, you will see God move!

Now, if you lead them through those two invitation questions and they don't respond, there is one more thing that you can ask them:

Now, if you lead them through those two invitation questions and they don't respond, there is one more thing that you can ask them:

Is there anything you would like me to pray for?

Often people are happy for you to pray for them, and it's an invitation that can lead them to experience the power and the presence of God at that moment.

Don't be afraid to pray for them in the moment and see what He will do. Ask them if anything has changed? Explain that it is because Jesus loves them.

You will be amazed at what can potentially open up from here for further conversation. If it's a general prayer, you can just ask Jesus to bless them. Finally, thank them for the opportunity and remind them that Jesus loves them.

THEY SAY YES TO JESUS? NOW WHAT?

HOW TO DO A SALVATION PRAYER

> *Then he brought them out and said, "Sirs, what must I do to be saved?" And they said, "Believe in the Lord Jesus, and you will be saved, you and your household."*
>
> **ACTS 16:30-31**

There is not a script for a prayer of salvation. It's an honest and heartfelt prayer that comes from understanding and articulating what you know.

The importance of prayer is not what is said as much as it is a heart's confession. These prayers may sound different each time and perhaps can be awkward or clumsy at times, but as long as it's a confession of their belief and confession of their belief and confession of their hearts – they are saved.

> *"If you confess with your mouth that Jesus is Lord and believe in your heart that God raised Him from the dead, you will be saved. For it is with the heart, one believes and is justified, and with the mouth, one confesses and is saved. The scripture says, "everyone who believes in Him will not be put to shame."* [1]
>
> **ROMANS 10:9-11**

FACILITATOR NOTES:

1. Break down Romans 10:9-11 and focus on the things we need to do to be saved. What do unbelievers need to acknowledge? What do they need to confess?

There are four things a person needs to do to receive Christ:

- Admit they're a sinner.
- Ask for forgiveness and turn away from sin (repentance).
- Believe that Jesus died on the cross and rose again for them.
- Receive Jesus Christ as Lord and Saviour into their heart and life

They can be confident if they do these things that they are saved and have received Jesus; they are assured of this through Romans 10:13 which says:

"Whoever calls upon the name of the Lord will be saved."

Here's a sample prayer you can pray to receive Christ:

"Dear Lord Jesus, I know I am a sinner, and I ask for your forgiveness. I believe you died for my sins and rose from the dead. I trust and follow you as my Lord and Saviour. Guide my life and help me to follow after you. In Jesus' name, amen."

FACILITATOR NOTES:

1. Go through the salvation prayer together and then break into pairs. Ask participants to go through a salvation prayer with each other.

QUESTIONS:

What are some ways that God has impacted you that you could share in telling your story? How can your audience connect with this?

What are the four simple things you can do in 'Your role' in sharing Jesus confidently?

How has Jesus been the solution in the situation to point someone to Jesus?

© Sharee Rice

QUESTIONS:

Share some of the ways you have learnt to engage someone for a response?

What are the four things a person needs to do to receive Christ?

Discuss the importance of the four steps one can take once they have said Yes to Jesus?
(Tell someone, read the bible, pray, connect).

FAQ

FREQUENTLY ASKED QUESTIONS

FACILITATOR TIPS

SESSION 05
KEY FOCUSES

WHILST SESSION 5 IS TITLED "FAQS", IT HAS A SPECIFIC FOCUS ON THE FOLLOWING:

- Understanding the obstacles which restrict us from sharing our faith
- Understanding how to deal with fear
- Understanding how to deal with rejection
- Knowing what to do next

TIP 1

Introduce session 5 as the concluding session. Reflect back on the first 4 session and tie it all into the final part. I.e., "In the first 4 sessions we covered what to say, how to say it, as well as the role of both God and man. But sometimes we are hindered by our own fears and past rejections. In this session we will learn how to overcome...".

TIP 2

Invite people to speak into what hinders them from sharing the Gospel. This will be a good way to gauge areas you can speak into/moments to pause.

TIP 3

Activity Have everyone visit the Engel scale in chapter 5. Get them to evaluate where they are, as well as where they believe their friends and family may be. It is a great tool to show your group that they can't fail at sharing the gospel! Re-instate this over and over!

TIP 4

You'll notice that 2 Timothy 1:7 is stated 3 times in session 5. This is intentional. Highlighting this passage throughout the chapter will continually remind participants of biblical truth.

TIP 5

Reflect on course Ask your group what was something that they took away from the course, or what marked them. Ask everyone to fill out the course feedback. Filter this through to your oversight!

ADDITIONAL EXERCISES/PRAYER TOPICS

• Pray for fear of man to be broken off people's lives; declare a healthy fear of the Lord

• Have your group record their testimonies from the weeks of doing the course/any experiences or encounters they may have had due to SJC, and send to **sjc@shareerice.com**

© Sharee Rice

1. WHAT ARE SOME OF THE OBSTACLES WE FACE IN SHARING OUR FAITH?

Sharing our faith is challenged by a number of obstacles, but to summarize them all, one word is "fear".

COMMON STAGES OF LIFE:

1. LOOK TO SOCIAL IMPROVEMENTS
Life needs are not met by social improvement, affluence or materialism. People may seek positions of power, status, relationships or possessions to answer this desire.

2. HAVE AN INTERNAL EMPTINESS
People try to fill the void through a number of different avenues like substance abuse, addictions, overworking and relationships.

3. ARE LONELY
You can be in a crowd of people and still feel lonely. Everyone is searching for a deeper sense of connection, community and a Saviour.

4. HAVE A FEAR OF DEATH
There is a universal fear of death – The question that arises: What's on the other side? Everyone is seeking assurance of what awaits them on the other side of death.

"Jesus explains in Matthew 10:16-33 that we will face persecution when sharing the gospel, which causes some to feel fear. In fact, he says we will be like sheep among the wolves, which probably should elicit a sense of fear in some people. Yet Jesus encourages us not to fear, to fear God, not what man can do to kill the body, but rather what God can do to kill the soul. That is comforting and profound in bringing our sense of fear into perspective, so from here we will look how to deal with fear".

You may also find that sharing your faith is easier when you realize that everyone goes through similar experiences in life.

FACILITATOR NOTES:

1. What other things do people look to in life? For example, they may not want to believe because they think they will 'miss out' on certain things.

© Sharee Rice

FAQ

2 DEALING WITH FEAR

"For God gave us a spirit not of fear but of power and love and self-control."
2 TIMOTHY 1:7

What we FEAR controls us and holds us back. Scripture encourages us to fear God and fear Him only.

WHAT IS FEAR?
False. **E**vidence. **A**ppearing. **R**eal.

We all at some point have fears around:
- What if I?
- How will it affect me?
- What if they reject me?
- What if I fail in sharing?

The Bible tells us in Hebrews 13:5

I will never leave you nor forsake you.

The great thing about sharing is that you can't actually fail!

That's right! Every time you speak to someone about Jesus it's a time in their day when they are at least thinking of Jesus that they otherwise wouldn't be and the Engle scale shows us that we are moving people one step closer to Jesus through these interactions.

FACILITATOR NOTES: PAGES 76-77

1. What kinds of things do we feel when we have a sense of fear in a situation or if we avoid talking about Jesus in a situation?

2. Explain and go over the Engle scale with your group. If unsure, have a look at it in detail and ask someone to explain it to you.

ENGEL SCALE MEANS YOU CAN'T FAIL
ENGEL SCALE - STAGES OF BELIEF

-10	Awareness of the supernatural
-9	No effective knowledge of Christianity
-8	Initial awareness of Christianity
-7	Interest in Christianity
-6	Aware of basic facts of the Gospel
-5	Grasp of implications of the Gospel
-4	Positive attitude towards the Gospel
-3	Awareness of personal need
-2	Challenge and decision to act
-1	Repentance and faith
0	A Disciple is Born!
+1	Evaluation of decision
+2	Initiation to the church
+3	Become part of the process of making other disciples
+4	Growth in understanding of the faith
+5	Growth in Christian character
+6	Discovery and use of gifts
+7	Christian Life-Style
+8	Stewardship of resources
+9	Prayer
+10	Openess to Others / Effective sharing of faith and life

Therefore - plan for success, not failure.
"If you fail to plan, then you plan to fail."

3 FEAR OF REJECTION

While you can't 'fail in sharing' you can be rejected, so the question is:

How do we deal with rejection?
Rejection is based on a fear of man.

WHAT DOES THE BIBLE SAY ABOUT REJECTION?

MATTHEW 19:16-30
The story of the rich man
Jesus never chased anyone, appeased anyone, adjusted His message for anyone, nor was He quiet in His approach.

"For am I now seeking the approval of man, or of God? Or am I trying to please man? If I were still trying to please man, I would not be a servant of Christ."
GALATIANS 1:10

"For God gave us a spirit not of fear but of power and love and self-control."
2 TIMOTHY 1:7

We can learn **how to deal with fear of rejection** from the life of Paul that we see in the book of Acts.

FACILITATOR NOTES:
1. Go through these bible verses above together with your group.

ACTS 17 Paul preached the good news, it was not received by people, and Paul was rejected and sometimes chased from towns.

V1-9 Paul persuaded some people to faith in Jesus but others formed a mob, attacked the house where Paul stayed, and moved Paul on.

V10 - 15 Many believed, but some came agitating and stirring up the crowds. They moved Paul on.

V16 - 21 He reasoned in the synagogue, some philosopher's conversed, "what does this babbler wish to say?"

V22- 34 Paul addresses them and unknown gods. Now when they heard of the resurrection, some mocked, but some believed.

So you keep doing what you know to do; care and share.

REMEMBER:

IF THEY REJECT JESUS, THEY ARE NOT REJECTING YOU. IF THEY ACCEPT JESUS, THEY ARE NOT ACCEPTING YOU.

HOW TO DEAL WITH REJECTION

But when you are processing that sense of rejection, personally, it is essential to:

1. Acknowledge emotions
They are real, and process those with the Holy Spirit.

> *I have not given you a spirit of fear but of love, power, and a sound mind.*
> 1 TIMOTHY 2:7

2. It doesn't define you or what you say.
It's one person's opinion, learn from it.

3. Examine what they rejected.
Don't criticise yourself but examine. Learn from the moment of interaction and be grateful for it.

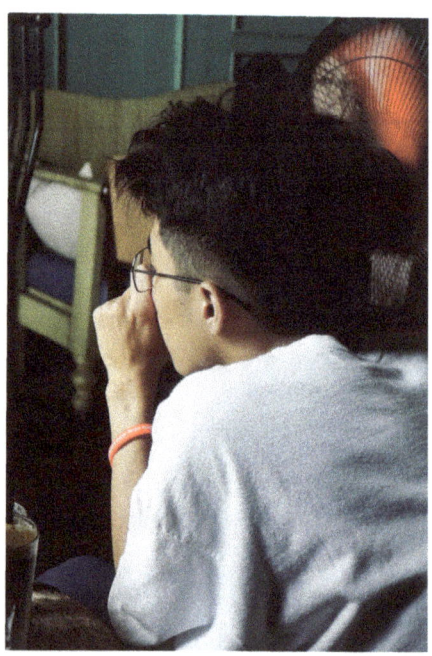

4 FEAR OF NOT KNOWING ENOUGH

God will give you what you need to say.

This is a very common fear, and we have all felt like this at some stage. But the Bible says that God will give us what we need to say, and also says that we don't need to be anxious.

Don't be anxious about how you should defend yourself or what you should say, for the Holy Spirit will teach you in that very hour what you ought to say.[1]

LUKE 12:12

HOW TO DEAL WITH NOT KNOWING ENOUGH?

Focus your conversation on Jesus. Trust that God will give you the words to speak.

DON'T BE AFRAID OF SAYING "I DON'T KNOW".

Say, "I don't know, I will get back to you", then get back to them. Focus your conversation on Jesus.

FACILITATOR NOTES:

1. Read Luke 12:12 with your group. Encourage them in this area. Use a personal example or ask someone if they have experienced God giving them what to say in a situation.

5. WHAT DO I NEED TO DO ONCE THEY ARE SAVED?

GET THEM STARTED ON THEIR JOURNEY:

Congratulate them on the decision they've made, and express how you would love to get them started in being a follower of Jesus.

Follow these steps:

1. Tell someone
Encourage them to speak to someone about the decision they've made. It's important they start talking about it and the life-changing experience they have had.

2. Read the Bible
God wants to speak to them – encourage them to download the 'YouVersion' Bible App. If they are looking where to start, you can encourage them to start in the book of John or the book of Mark.

3. Pray
Encourage them to pray. God wants to speak to them and for them to speak to God each day. He is willing to listen if they are willing to talk.

4. Connect
Connect them with other Christian's. It's important they have other believers around them to help grow their relationship with God. Connect them with a local church and people through Life Groups. It is an essential part of being a follower of Jesus.

FACILITATOR NOTES:

1. Ask if anyone has experienced taking someone through the salvation prayer. Encourage your group to share how someone helped them on their own journey after the point of salvation.

QUESTIONS:

What are the three enemies of sharing Jesus confidently?

What are some things you can do to overcome fear?

What are four things that God will do when you don't feel like you have enough to share?

QUESTIONS:

What are some things we need to remember if we are feeling a sense of rejection?

CONGRATULATIONS!

WE ARE SO GLAD YOU HAVE COMPLETED THE SHARING JESUS CONFIDENTLY COURSE. OUR PRAYER FOR YOU IS THAT THIS HAS EQUIPPED YOU TO GO OUT AND SHARE THE GOOD NEWS OF JESUS IN YOUR SCHOOLS, FRIEND CIRCLES, SPORTING GROUPS, AND ANYWHERE GOD PLACES YOU! WE WOULD LOVE TO HEAR YOUR TESTIMONIES AND FEEDBACK FROM THIS COURSE.

PLEASE EMAIL US AT SJC@SHAREERICE.COM

OR YOU CAN SHARE YOUR STORIES ON INSTAGRAM AND ADD #SJC.

www.ingramcontent.com/pod-product-compliance
Lightning Source LLC
Chambersburg PA
CBHW040242010526
44107CB00065B/2850